Cover design, music, edited by Thomm Morgan
First printing: April 2012

Library of Congress Control Number: 2012905533
ISBN: Hardcover   978-1-4691-8608-5
               Softcover   978-1-4691-8607-8
               Ebook   978-1-4691-8609-2

To order additional copies of this book, contact:
Xlibris Corporation
1-888-795-4274
www.Xlibris.com
Orders@Xlibris.com
112136

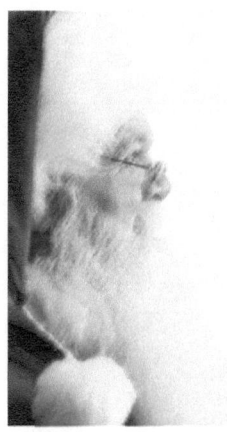

SANTA CLAUS IN LAUGHING VALLEY

A Christmas Fantasy
And a call for parents to fight for the arts in public schools

Teresa deBarba-Miller
Cover design, music, edited by Thomm Morgan
The Value of Participatory Storytelling by Laura Simms

Dedication

Dedicated to *The Agape Choir*, now performing in the area of St. Louis, Missouri.

Teresa says, "Never before, entering ninety years of life, have I come across a bunch of individuals so *radiant*, so *loving*, so *magnetic*, so *utterly sincere* as those who function as *the Agape Choir*!

"Individual by individual—founders, leaders, and instructors alike—they truly believe that love of one is love of another and another and another, until all humanity is embraced and the heavenly city realized.

"Long may they live in their chosen fields of endeavor.

"Long may they continue to perform, spreading *joy* whenever/wherever they appear—*the Agape Choir*!"

For details, contact **Pooki@GatewaytoAgape.com**.

In Appreciation

First, my thanks to master storymentor, teacher, and humanitarian Laura Simms for showing us the value of participatory storytelling. I encourage any storyteller to visit **www.LauraSimms.com** to learn more about Laura.

Repeated thanks to Thomm Morgan, who provided speedy editing, many suggestions, cover designs, and music along the way to seeing this book published. Thanks, Thomm!

This work would never have progressed without the help of computer assistants. First, Amy McNeely, who typed and typed before she left to finish her college degree. Second (mostly), Karen Luter, who came to my rescue after Amy left. She also typed plenty before leaving to begin a new career as a teacher. Appreciation also to "the other Amy," Amy Rhoades, who put finishing touches and polish on Thomm's edits.

The copyeditor for the publisher definitely must be recognized as well. Cleofe Marie Faelnar certainly exceeded expectations with fantastic critiques and suggestions before the final galleys were submitted.

And thank you, dear reader. You are the reason I write, in hopes that something I have learned in my eighty-nine years will be passed along.

As you will soon see, without assistance, I venture nowhere.

Contents

BIOGRAPHIES

The Value of Participatory Storytelling

Laura Simms

I have had the distinct pleasure of creating tales with audiences young and old for years. Repeatedly, in situations that might be impossible (distractions, discipline problems, unsuitable environment for storytelling), it has always been the telling of a "joining in" story that would break the ice and bring the audience together in a dynamic and fruitful listening.

The tradition of participation stories is ageless and known to most cultures. A storytelling occasion can include spoken, sung, or incanted words; dance; songs; sound effects; poetry; call and response; and theater and musical accompaniment. Such events are considered vital to the health of individuals, the community, and the environment. Some of the benefits of this style of performance include bringing people together; engendering happiness; instilling social responsibility; heightening awareness, synchronizing mind and body; and renewing one's sense of sacred in the everyday world.

The energy stimulated in reciprocal activity was like a wellspring. Our ears finally tuned and taught us how to listen carefully and viscerally to any tale, whether it included outward response or not. When the storyteller invites the listener to reverberate the sounds of the story, the audiences' combined answer is stronger than any individual's answer. Harnessed to the story by the presence of the teller, we could whinny and neigh and ride freely in response. At the same time, we had the delightful satisfaction of consciously supporting the creation of the event. It is well worth the extra effort.

I learned a great deal from experience. I began to incorporate songs, gestures, and hand clapping in my stories with the young students. My acceptance and utilization of their input made them eager to hear more stories and to write their own. Also, I learned that although my audience was more than willing to take part, it was up to me to make the right invitation and up to me to keep the integrity of the story forthcoming. If I had memorized the story with gestures and repeated it by rote rather than by heart, I would lose my connection with them. Their response would be halfhearted because they knew I was more involved with my story than with the one we were making together. My telling always had to be fresh. In other words, I had to know my story well but be open to accept their responses as well as orchestrate them so the whole situation worked.

The awareness and vitality that is called for on the part of the teller is a particularly challenging task for a beginner. You might ask, how can you learn a story by heart and not by rote? First of all, in live performance, the words are only one part of the story. The meaning and intention and the breath and response of the teller is another, while the imaginative and psychological response of the audience is the jewel.

The experience of participation truly generates happiness. When we concentrate on the story and become responsible for bringing it alive, it takes us out of the concerns we have in our everyday life. There is renewed creative energy to find alternative ideas and meaning in one's life. The sound of the stories reconnects us to the song inherent in everything. And perhaps one benefit, which we usually associate with the content of the story rather than the act of telling it, is that joining in generates social responsibility by reminding us we are able to respond.

Participatory storytelling where audiences are engaged and responding is more needed now than ever before. It is our role as storytellers and caring adults to create situations for our children where reciprocity, embodied listening, and capacity for inner joy and imagination can antidote the disconnection that digital, more passive involvement engenders. Telling a story is medicine and practice in being a full human being.

Copyright © 2012 by Laura Simms

*This introduction was condensed from the introduction to **Joining In: An Anthology of Audience Participation Stories & How to Tell Them** (Yellow Moon Press, Cambridge, MA).

Santa Claus in Laughing Valley

Before he moved to the North Pole, Santa lived in a place called Laughing Valley inside a magnificent castle where his toys were made.

Storyteller: Optional music with lyrics is found after the story.

He had the same helpers, same elves, same fairies. Just like now, they were busy as could be from the beginning of the year to the eve of December 24, when all the toys were delivered by Santa in a huge sleigh pulled by his reindeer across the sky from chimney to chimney. You know that story, right? Oh, come on, sure you do!

> *(Use this opportunity to converse with your audience in a Hans Andersen type of banter. [See notes] You may remind them about heralded stories like "Rudolph the Red-Nosed Reindeer" and such or whatever your listeners tell you of more appropriate musical or film reminders. Return to your story.)*

After all the toys and gifts were delivered on Christmas Eve, what do you suppose Santa and his helpers did? Care to guess what they did?

(Wait to see if any hands are raised. If not, tell them.)

Why, they took a week's vacation!

Between December 26 and January 2, they learned pretty much about everything that happened here on earth. Boy, they talked and listened to everybody's business!

Then on January 3, it was back to work, starting from scratch to make toys and gifts for the following Christmas. That's how they lived, from year to year and from century to century, in Laughing Valley. They loved it there. They called it Laughing Valley because everyone living there was happy and gay.

The valley cradled a brook that actually chuckled as it went its way along. As for the wind, you never heard it howling in Laughing Valley! No. It merely whistled merrily through the trees, making the prettiest kind of music. Sunbeams danced lightly over the soft grass with patches of violets or other beautiful wildflowers smiling up from their green nest of leaves. People laughed a lot because everyone was happy.

Everyone in Laughing Valley fully expected to keep on doing exactly what they did each year—being perfectly happy forever and ever. Like Santa himself.

All of a sudden, everything changed. Who can predict change? And such a drastic change! New neighbors moved into the caves located on the north side of Laughing Valley. They made their homes not far from each other in caves inside Shadow Mountain. They looked like ordinary human beings. They could have been your neighbor.

It might have worked out okay, but much of the material Santa's elves used for toys was gathered below Shadow Mountain in the deep forest beyond the caves. These new neighbors hated the daily intrusions into "their territory."

And so it was that unlikely things, unwelcome things, began to occur. For example, nearly invisible wires would mysteriously appear across stairs in the castle or in doorways, which tripped the elves.

(Can you guess a few other so-called accidents? Wait for two or three suggestions to be offered. Three is maximum. Pick up your story after that. If no suggestions are forthcoming, make up a few "accidents" of your own. Now back to our story.)

The fairies who flew everywhere reported that it was their new neighbors who were causing the many, many bandages seen on almost everyone.

Now you would think that good old Santa Claus and his helpers, who devote every single day toward making children and adults happy, would have no enemies anywhere on earth. As a matter of fact, for years on end, he had encountered only love wherever they went. Santa knew that nothing is more essential than giving and receiving true love.

However, the cave dwellers proved to be a breed of really miserable beings, a type of human entirely unknown to the other occupants of Laughing Valley.

You could never guess what made them so miserable, so I'll tell you. It was Santa Claus himself! Can you guess why?

(Care to try a few more guesses here? If you hit a blank stare, go right on.)

Easy. Remember, Santa was chief honcho! It was by following his leadership that made the regular residents so happy!

The fact is those five miserable guys—the new residents—happened to be real demons! They did not *want* anybody to be happy, especially not children.

The oldest demon, biggest of the five, lived in a cave at the foot of Shadow Mountain. I guess you could call him, quite honestly, Demon **Selfish**! Alongside his home was another cave occupied by Demon **Envy**. Behind that, another cave belonged to Demon **Hatred**. Beyond that, in the very heart of the mountain, one could find the dark and fearful cave of Demon **Evil**.

Each of these four caves was connected by a narrow tunnel, which ultimately led to a fifth cave, a cozy little room occupied by a lonely guy named **Repentance**. Rocky floors on the passage leading to **Repentance** were worn smooth because people who visited the caves of the other demons had to pass through all four in order to visit **Repentance**.

*(Does everybody here know what the word **repentance** means? Wait for replies. If somebody guesses the verb **repent**, acknowledge with a big smile. If no replies are*

*offered, tell your audience that **repent** or **repentance** means to be sorry for something you have done or because you behaved badly and to change your ways.)*

Repentance actually had a reputation for being a pleasant kind of fellow who gladly opened his doors. If his visitor appeared to be *sincerely* sorrowful, he or she was ushered into fresh air and sunshine brightening the forest of flowers, plants, and other stuff gathered by Santa's elves on the other side of Shadow Mountain.

At first, the demons tried to make Santa and his helpers discontented. A temper tantrum, perhaps? Didn't work. All they got for their pathetic attempts were chuckles, out-and-out grins, and laughs left and right. Happiness, happiness—nothing but happiness remained everywhere in Laughing Valley.

How to burst those endless bubbles of glee? The demons decided to hold a meeting to discuss how to get rid of Santa Claus once and for all. By now, they really hated him. And you know why, right?

(Look around. If you notice doubt on your audiences' faces, go on.)

Well, let me tell you why. Picture yourself at a meeting. One of those miserable guys is talking.

"I'm really getting lonesome," said Demon **Selfish**. "Nobody comes to visit me, especially in December. And why? Because when people find out that Santa gives away all those pretty Christmas presents, they get the idea that to become happy and generous themselves, people should give things away. Nobody comes to visit me in December!"

Demon **Envy** added, "I'm having the same trouble. Nobody gets jealous in December. It seems the whole world is busy guessing what will be received, or deciding what will be given to other people. I can't coax anyone to become *envious* in December."

"Well, I'm having the same trouble, too," announced Demon **Hatred**. "Now I understand why! If nobody passes through your caves, they surely cannot reach *mine*!"

"Nor mine!" added Demon **Malice**.

*(Have I not mentioned Demon **Malice**? Yes, yes, he's there too! **Malice** simply likes to see people suffer.)*

"For my part," uttered **Repentance**, "I can see that if children do not visit any of your caves, they surely have no need to pass through and visit me. I, too, feel every bit as neglected as you are feeling!"

"All this because of one person they call *Santa Claus*!" raged Demon **Envy**. "He is simply ruining our lives. Something must be done at once!"

They quickly agreed, but *what*? This was another matter entirely, much more difficult to settle. What to do? When to do it?

By this time, they had learned that Santa Claus worked all year long in Laughing Valley. They knew he never left home, not until Christmas Eve.

At first, they talked about trying to get him into their caves in order to push him into terrible pitfalls, which ended in destruction. It sounded good. And they tried it. What a laugh! Santa wouldn't think of changing his scheduled routine. Leave home? Never until Christmas Eve!

On another day while Santa was busy at work surrounded by his little band of happy assistants, Demon **Selfish** went right up to him and said, "These toys are so bright and pretty. Why don't you keep them? It's a pity to give them away to those noisy boys and fretful girls who break or destroy them quickly!"

"Nonsense!" bellowed Santa, his bright eyes twinkling merrily as he turned toward the tempter. "Once they have my presents, the boys and girls stop being noisy and fretful. If I can make them happy one day of the year, I am quite content."

Selfish went back to the others, moaning, "I have failed. I have failed. Santa Claus does not have a selfish bone in his whole body."

"Let me try," said **Envy**.

So Demon **Envy** visited Santa. Right off the bat, in a positive manner, he said, "The toy shops are full of things every bit as appealing as the toys and gifts you make. Today, people use machines which spill out goods much faster than you could ever make them by hand. They sell them for money while you get nothing at all for your work. What a shame!"

11

Santa Claus refused to be envious of the business shops. "Oh, it's a fine thing they do," he answered. "I can supply the big and little people only once a year—on Christmas Eve. The businesspeople bring much happiness to my friends all year 'round. I like businesspeople! I am glad to see them prosper!"

Silence. Huge silence. What now?

At the next meeting, **Hatred** spoke up. "Well, it's my turn!" He really thought he could influence Santa Claus! He bustled around a busy workshop, announcing importantly, "Good morning, Santa, I have bad news for you."

"Then run away, like a good fellow," said Santa Claus. "Bad news is something that should be kept secret and not discussed in public."

Now what?! Oh, they were persistent, those demons!

All together they visited him, thinking to gang up on him with logic. A different voice punctuated each remark, one uttered immediately after another:

"You cannot escape this!"

"Admit it!"

"In this world, most people do not believe in Santa Claus!"

"Some hate you bitterly!"

"Stuff and nonsense!" replied Santa. "You're so silly! Don't you know that to hate anyone is the same as feeding yourself poison? Hate is someone else's concern, not mine. *I don't hate a soul, not a soul!*"

Giving his famous chuckle—"HO HO HO!"—he put his kiss of approval on a darling little doll, handing it to an elf, who placed it in a room filling up with toys to deliver on Christmas Eve.

As I told you, the demons did not give up easily. They tried other ways to tempt old Santa Claus. Shrewd enough to see they wanted only mischief and trouble, Santa simply ignored them.

Finally, the demons' time had come. They honestly felt they *had* to rid the world of Santa Claus! They *had* to! If not, they would surely die of sheer loneliness. *They were not prepared to die so young of such a terrible death. Abominable!*

They understood that no harm could reach Santa while he lived in Laughing Valley. Too many elves and fairies were around to protect him. However, he must *leave* the valley on Christmas Eve to drive his sleigh around the world!

AHA! They must concoct—prepare somehow—a slow-acting poison! After all, didn't Santa himself mention *poison* in the first place? They needed to find a way to sneak it in and feed it *to the reindeer* just before they were due to leave on Christmas Eve! When the deer were flying high in the sky, the poison would become active enough to kill them all, and Santa Claus too! Along with toys and gifts, they would all smash down to earth and be shattered!

It sounded so easy! The demons hugged each other (they had never done that before!) and ran around laughing. For the first time in their lives, they actually *laughed*. *Big mistake!*

Do you remember what Peter Pan had experienced? When an unexpected laugh broke into a thousand pieces, each piece went skipping about, inviting ever so many more laughs!

Instead of figuring out what the poison itself should be and how to feed it to the reindeer, the demons found themselves looking at each other and laughing again. *Uproariously*! Could it be laughter that did it? Maybe it was the hugs exchanged in their glee at having hit upon a solution! No matter.

Something miraculous happened! The surprising, amazing miracle of laughter grabbed every one of them. They actually enjoyed it! They enjoyed the hugs being exchanged! They enjoyed being happy! What a weird experience!

I'll bet you can tell me what happened next. Come on, tell me what *you* guess happened next.

(Acknowledge suggestions from your audience in your most serious manner, no matter what is offered. Make it all okay. You may have to stretch your imagination more than usual, but you can do it! End with a good laugh by all.)

Note to storyteller: After reading *The Complete Illustrated Stories of Hans Christian Andersen* (Chancellor Press), which includes his own autobiography "The Story of My Life," and after reading various reviews of musical productions, I remain perplexed. Somewhere in my memory exist the words of an unknown storyteller who claimed Andersen to be the first to introduce "audience participation" to his audiences. That made eminent sense. I could easily imagine this world-acclaimed "writer, actor, and singer of songs" bringing people to share some of his stories with him.

Of course, this may also have been said by someone who attended Diane Wolkstein's Saturday morning summer appearances with other storytellers in Central Park, New York City, telling stories in an alcove in front of a huge statue of Mr. Andersen. Being privileged to be one of the storytellers there, those few years with the New York City Storytelling Center remain a treasured memory.

Storytelling as an Art

Storytelling was revived in the 1970s as an American art form under the leadership of Jimmy Neil Smith and many, many storytelling friends. Today, Jimmy is recognized as the founder and president emeritus of the International Storytelling Center. (**www.storytellingcenter.net**)

Storytelling—be it participatory or simply told as a true story, fiction, or fairy tale, whether based on religion, a legend, a myth, or folktale, etc.—is only one of many "arts" that should be taught in public schools in every state, particularly from first grade through adolescent years.

All arts, especially when taught to youngsters, gives full scope to creating successful, imaginative human beings.

Storytellers around the World

Storyteller	—America	Goze	—Japan
Bard	—Celtic	Rhapsode	—Greece
Minstrel	—France	Seanchai	—Ireland
Troubadour	—France	Ustad	—Afghanistan
Raconteur	—France	Amauta	—Peru
Gleoman	—England	Cuentista	—Spanish
Dasarula	—India	Cantor de Feria	—Spain
Bhopi	—India	Kontu Kantari	—Basque
Gusliari	—Russia	Marchen	—Italy
Gosan	—Persia	Tohunga	—Polynesia
Etoki Hoshi	—Japan	Liedjesznger	—Holland
Manteur	—Haitian Creole		
Pevci	—Southern Slavic		

SANTA'S LAUGHING SONG

Based on the story by Teresa deBarba-Miller | 2012 © Thomm Morgan

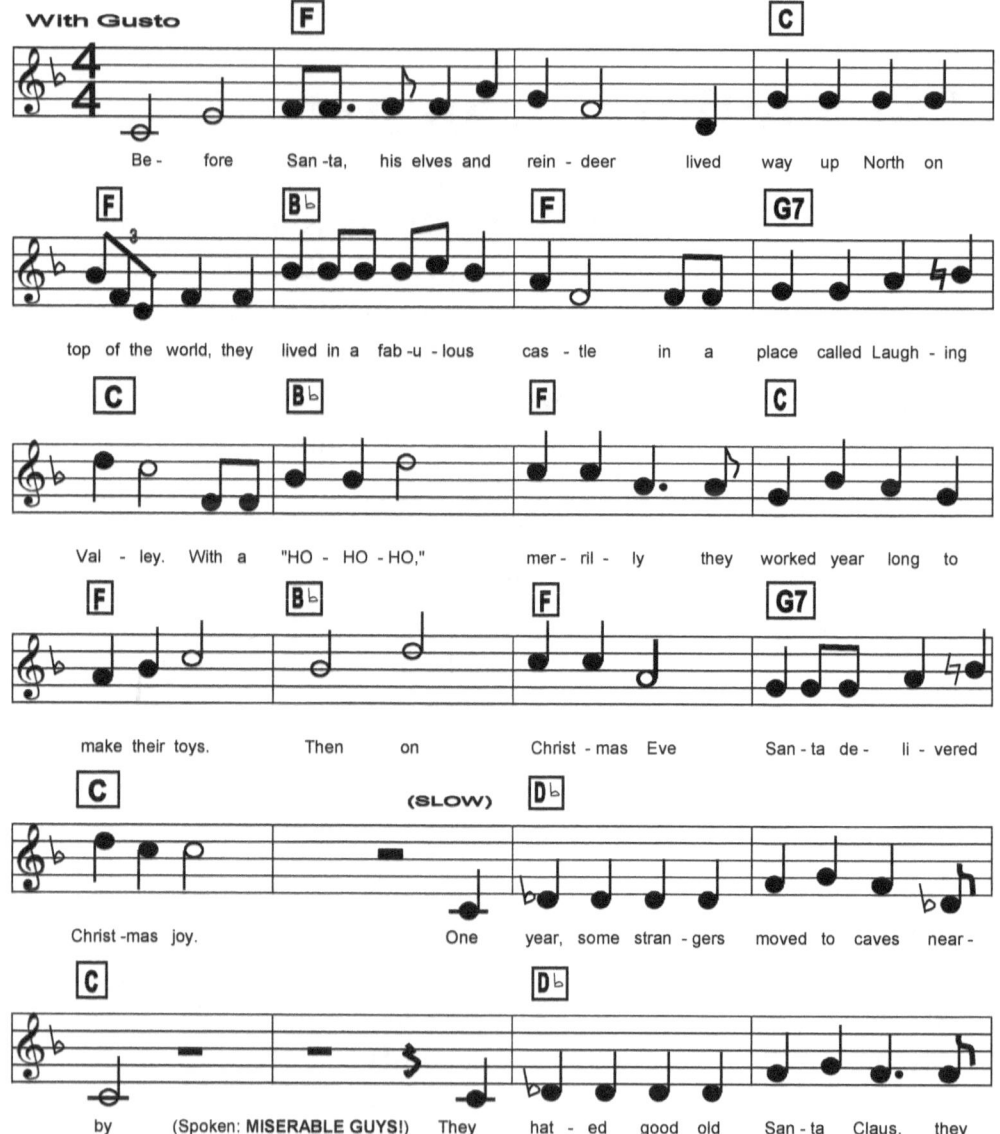

With Gusto

F ... C
Be - fore San -ta, his elves and rein - deer lived way up North on

F ... Bb ... F ... G7
top of the world, they lived in a fab-u-lous cas -tle in a place called Laugh - ing

C ... Bb ... F ... C
Val - ley. With a "HO - HO - HO," mer - ril - ly they worked year long to

F ... Bb ... F ... G7
make their toys. Then on Christ - mas Eve San - ta de - li - vered

C ... (SLOW) ... Db
Christ -mas joy. One year, some stran - gers moved to caves near-

C ... Db
by (Spoken: **MISERABLE GUYS!**) They hat - ed good old San - ta Claus, they

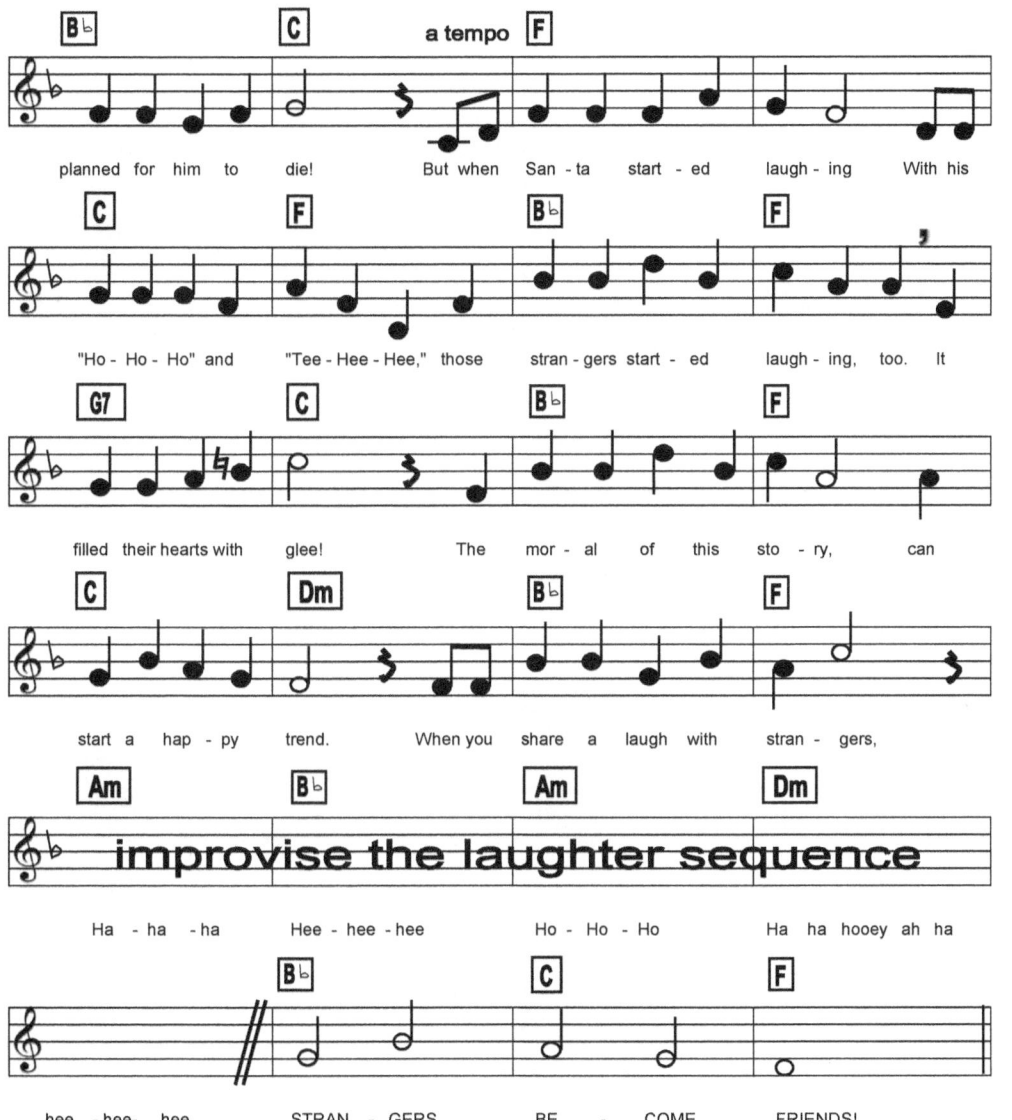

Bb   C   a tempo   F

planned for him to die!   But when San - ta start - ed laugh - ing   With his

C   F   Bb   F

"Ho - Ho - Ho" and "Tee - Hee - Hee," those stran - gers start - ed laugh - ing, too.   It

G7   C   Bb   F

filled their hearts with glee!   The mor - al of this sto - ry, can

C   Dm   Bb   F

start a hap - py trend.   When you share a laugh with stran - gers,

Am   Bb   Am   Dm

improvise the laughter sequence

Ha - ha - ha   Hee - hee - hee   Ho - Ho - Ho   Ha ha hooey ah ha

Bb   C   F

hee - hee - hee   STRAN - GERS   BE - COME   FRIENDS!

Preface to Part Two

You remember the title of this book includes ". . . and *a Call for Every Parent to Fight for the Arts in Public Schools.*"

Having read and heard about so many of the arts being cut from schools as budgets are slashed, I became quite perturbed, and started a dialogue with someone who has a PhD in educational administration. (She asked to remain anonymous.)

Said I, *"As a child of immigrant parents, I remember public schools teaching every known art. Musicians in our own orchestra, stage plays for each grade in front of a sizable audience, poetry, art lessons—name it, we had it all. Today, it seems only charter schools, private schools, and better public schools enjoy this kind of education. Where did society slip up?"*

My advisor immediately straightened me out. *"Education is the responsibility of the states. Many states have legislation regarding the arts."*

Looking back, matter of fact, we did not "have it all." My life would have gone completely otherwise had we been instructed during adolescence in the ways of the human reproduction system, to say nothing of sex (a different subject). In the twenties (I am now eighty-nine years old), there was no such thing as kindergarten. I went into first grade. I think it was in the eighth grade that they brought out a frog, and we dissected it. That was the extent of my education in biology.

My experience as a storyteller, in my sixties, completely altered my world view.

I vividly recall working pro bono (for the public good, without fee), where I appeared as a storyteller in New York City and Nassau County public schools. I watched children as their imaginations took flight as I told them stories. Now it seems "the arts" are slipping into the dark shadows of "Budget-Cut Valley."

Can we find a way to surmount this dismal situation?

> Every bit as valuable as providing proper nutrition to stimulate your brain activity is stimulating your intelligence with imagination.

Professional storytelling is only one of many arts out there. In my business dealings, there were ample opportunities for me to meet memorable individuals. One of these was Padraic Colum, a famous Irish poet, novelist, dramatist, biographer, children's book author, and collector of folklore. Said he,

> *Imagination is one of the great faculties common to all exceptional people—to soldiers, statesmen, saints, to artist, scientist, philosophers and great business men. Imagination is the beginning of creation. As George Bernard Shaw said, "You imagine what you desire;*

you will what you can imagine and at last you create what you will."

Among Albert Einstein's famous quotes are the following: (If you don't know who he is, I surrender!)

- *"Imagination is more important than knowledge."*
- *"Logic will get you from A to B. Imagination will take you everywhere."*
- *"Imagination is <u>everything</u>. It is the preview of life's coming attractions."*
- *"Imagination is more important than knowledge. For knowledge is limited to all we know and understand, while imagination embraces the entire world, and all there ever will be to know and understand."*
- *"Imagination provides the ability to grasp higher mathematics. Think of the imagination as a muscle. In very young children, it's healthy, flexible, joyfully exercised. As we grow older, it becomes weak, even atrophied. Yet, imagination holds the key to making life choices, to inspire students to value their dreams, to RISK achieving significant things."*

According to First Lady Michelle Obama,

"The arts are not just a nice thing to have to do if there is free time or if one can afford it . . . Paintings

and poetry, music and design . . . they all define who
we are as a people."

I honestly believe that a proper arts program in all schools should emphasize, rather than minimize, the known arts as well as creative skills. I also believe that education must incorporate environmental studies to advance our students into thinking, imaginative human beings in every regard.

While cramming young brains full of facts about science and technology, what's wrong with creating successful human beings? What's wrong with having Friday afternoons devoted to the arts and discoveries needed for human advancement?

Cable TV, C-SPAN, July 17, 2011: Watching this broadcast raised my hackles. Introduced as one of the nation's foremost thinkers, Thomas Friedman, Foreign Affairs columnist for the *New York Times*, addressed the annual meeting of the National Governors Association.

Friedman first spoke of a new book he wrote with Michael Mandelbaum, ***That Used to Be Us: How America Fell Behind in the World It Invented and How We Can Come Back*** (Farrar, Straus, and Giroux.) Then came the zinger! He had just returned from China. He couldn't get over the progress he had just observed. *Eight months* in the making, from start to finish, the Chinese had completed a brand-new technological building, the most modern convention center you could imagine. He compared their speedy project completion to a broken escalator in a Washington, DC, building, which *had not been fixed for years*!

Here is Friedman's assessment on globalization and technology in what has become a hyperconnected world:

> *We must adapt, invent, and re-invent. We need individuals and companies <u>with high imagination</u> to keep abreast of China's progress, and the progress of every other forward-thinking nation. (Underlining is mine.)*

In other words, school education must emphasize that <u>higher imagination</u> needs to be a priority. That, my friends, means paying attention to the next section, a call to restore all the arts in every school, particularly those currently referred to as underserved!

As if I needed more ammunition, I want to mention another C-SPAN program memorializing Dr. Martin Luther King Jr. None of us oldsters could imagine the actualization of his speech, "I Have a Dream." Yet it did happen! Dr. King had to *imagine* it first! Not only has his birthday become a national holiday, but have you seen the huge monument erected in Washington, DC, or photographs of it? He looks down now on everybody who once called him boy, as people did for years.

As another aside, there are still those among us who object to a dark skin no matter who wears it. I wonder how long it will take the population at large to realize that the workings of one's *brain* mean more than any skin color or speech.

Please understand I'm all for science and technology! Who has not applauded the well-known genius of Steve Jobs, whose inventions still bear fruit? Steven Miller is another genius known only to a few in his immediate circle of peers. His remarkable imagination produced enough patented inventions to create yet another billionaire. I know because he happens to be my grandson, enjoying his wealth in Florida.

Again on cable TV, which feeds my observations (remember Einstein, *"Imagination will take you everywhere"*), I saw an infomercial showing how ergonomics works. For those not familiar with the term, The International Ergonomics Association defines *ergonomics* as follows:

> *Ergonomics [or human factors] is the scientific discipline concerned with the understanding of interactions among humans and other elements of a system, and the profession that applies theory, principles, data and methods to design in order to optimize human well-being and overall system performance.*

The commercial I saw depicted one lone individual moving unwieldy objects like a full-sized sofa, piano, bureau of drawers by using the inventor's *imaginative* design. The key words were *move and slide*, using the inventor's design underneath the object.

You will find examples of the power of imagination in every direction you choose to look: north, south, east, west, up, down, and across. In Africa, a prime example is Nelson Mandela. The movie *Invictus* showed the prison cell that held his body hostage for years while his *imagination* roamed at will.

He exercised daily, visualized seeing "apartheid" removed. Now his vision is reality.

Even closer to home is the miracle that is Oprah Winfrey. Do you think she got her network, OWN, by snapping her fingers? It may seem that way, but no, she had to *imagine* it first.

I would venture to say that most of us Americans—whatever our country of origin—are basically good, decent people looking for security in our lives, in our future. How to get it? Personally, I found it first through professional storytelling in public schools.

In the spirit of shameless self-promotion, explained on page 313 in *Holiday Stories All Year Round: Audience Participation Stories and More Holiday Data* (Libraries Unlimited), I tell of when I watched professional storyteller Diane Wolkstein demonstrate how to prepare a story for audience participation. It proved to be an eye/mind/intuition-shattering event during an annual conference of the American Library Association (ALA) held one summer in New York City. By this time, I was a staunch member of the New York City Storytelling Center.

I was sixty years old but felt like twenty, just beginning to understand what life was all about thanks mostly to books by other professional storytellers sharing their knowledge of this particular art form. I gobbled like they were the rarest of chocolates . . . legends, myths, true stories, fiction, folk tales from various countries, et cetera. My passion was to find work as a professional storyteller.

I soaked in the value of all the arts while attending, as a storyteller, weekly sessions of a nine-month course at Teacher's College, Columbia University, NYC. In other classes, there were singers, drummers, dancers, mimes, musicians, jugglers, puppeteers, even those handling wild animals and little-known domestic animals.

There we all were, learning from our teachers and learning from each other. All of us hell-bent on demonstrating our skills and talents in places that could afford to hire visiting artists. At that time in our nation's history, the parent-teacher associations raised and provided funds for schools to use for this purpose. Can they still do this? Don't know.

I *do* know we should introduce our young children to skills and arts as a significant step toward waking up their imaginations. This will not only stimulate their imaginations but also develop their own self-awareness of their individual gifts!

Call to Action

When another friend described the content of a couple of books she had read and a documentary she had seen, my excitement grew even higher.

From Greg Mortenson and David Oliver Relin come a book entitled *Three Cups of Tea: One Man's Mission to Promote Peace . . . One School at a Time* (Viking Press). A map depicting the northern areas of Pakistan and neighbors became Greg Mortenson's mission. By tenacious effort and example, he demonstrated his way to fight terrorism and build goodwill between nations by establishing a school especially for girls, which has since been the impetus for more than 350 similar schools. How did he do it? With donated pennies from the world over.

Granted, Greg Mortenson is a rare individual coming from a unique family background. Nonetheless, he still is an *American* building over 350 schools for girls in *Afghanistan* with minimum funds! Greg went by the teaching of his heart—and his intuition. A Wisconsin school began the fund-raising with Pennies for Peace. **(www.penniesforpeace.org)**

I'm asking, "Where do you send your pennies?"

Davis Guggenheim's documentary, *Waiting For Superman,* introduced at the Sundance Film Festival in 2010 uses the stories of children in several cities to make the case that American public education is failing. These are available on DVD in stores, libraries, or Amazon.

Where *do you send your pennies?*

Lear's Magazine, no longer in publication, alas, in April 1992 published *"The Private Hell of Public Education"* by Bonnie Blodgett. If you can locate it, read every word.

Where *do you send your pennies?*

From courageous Korean-American educator, Michelle Rhee, comes Richard Whitmore's book, *The Bee Eater* (Jossey-Bass.) Michelle believes children attending a great school should be a matter of fact, not luck, that every family should be able to choose an excellent school. Says Michelle, *"America's schools are failing our kids. On this point, the data is clear. Real change requires a better system, one that puts students' needs before those of special interests or wasteful bureaucracy."* (**www. studentsfirst.org**)

When I consider her youth and sense of style, I predict you may be seeing someday a movie of Michelle Rhee's life.

One last time . . . Where *do* you *send your pennies*?

A Call to Action—from Movies

Movies, my first passion (going back to the 1930s), are a splendid way to introduce us to remarkable stories and individuals. I remember the following:

To Sir, with Love

An idealistic engineer trainee (played by Sidney Poitier) teaches a group of rambunctious white high school students from the slums of London's East End.

Mr. Holland's Opus

A frustrated composer (Richard Dreyfuss) finds fulfillment as a high school music teacher.

Remember the Titans

Tells the true story of a newly appointed African-American coach (played by Denzel Washington) and his high school team on their first season as a racially integrated unit.

Stand and Deliver

Tells the true story of Jaime Escalante (Edward James Olmos), the East Los Angeles math teacher at Garfield High School. He transformed the school's math curriculum and pushed his struggling students to master advanced math and science courses.

Lean On Me

The dedicated but tyrannical Joe Clark (Morgan Freeman) is appointed the principal of a decaying inner-city school, which he improves by using unusual methods.

No doubt, many other movies exist about extraordinary human beings creating different methods to reach the psyches of troubled teenagers in order to assure a more positive future for them. <u>Note</u>: Without the arts, none of these movies would exist, and they all began with the spade work of just one person—an imaginative individual!

It's probably unrealistic to believe that we will, in the foreseeable future, realize Buckminster Fuller's dream come true. In *his* dream, all humans on planet Earth would carry interplanetary passports. While I think that is a little farfetched, I do not know of it being engraved in stone that all human beings cannot be *free* in thought.

As I've become older and physically limited by not one but two strokes, I am more and more convinced that we are *all* free to think what we will. More than that, we are free to empower ourselves as individuals, to put at least a portion of our available energies toward bettering the human condition in all its present situations.

In the grand scheme of things, I am hopeful you, dear reader, now fully realize the vital importance of the big picture I am trying to paint for you. If not, please go back and read again the **Preface to Part Two** section of this book.

In my opinion, we really must better compete with other nations furthering their own individual causes by using the technology *we Americans invented*!

I have tried and tried and tried again to come up with a plan for all parents and grandparents to use in order to persuade the educational powers that be about the value of introducing all the arts to all the schools, particularly those underserved.

Listen. You can go crazy trying to research the right organizations to connect *your pennies* with! So many are convinced they are custodians of the vision which bridges the gap between individual action and optimum results.

The key words, again, become *individual action*. As reported, I have no definite plan to offer. However, all of us need to find a way for parents and grandparents to work on their own without joining any particular organization. In other words, *what steps can an individual take* right away to see the changes we all want occurring within the foreseeable future?

I personally do not know what you can do. But you do. I would like to hear about that.

You have now read the problem. Write your solution, keeping it under fifty words. Then e-mail your thoughts: **AllTheArts@ yahoo.com**. I hope to compile these solutions into a document to forward to the state arts councils throughout our nation. They will know what to do with this Call to Action.

A brief story (author unknown):

*This is about four people named **Everybody, Somebody, Anybody,** and **Nobody**. There was an important job to be done. **Everybody** was asked to do it. **Everybody** was sure **Somebody** would do it. **Anybody** could have done it, but **Nobody** did! **Somebody** got angry about that because it was **Everybody's** job. **Everybody** thought **Anybody** would have done it, since **Anybody** could do it. **Nobody** realized that it was simply not done by **Anybody,** nor by **Somebody**. It ended up that **Everybody** blamed **Somebody! Nobody** did what **Anybody** could have done.*

As I approach ninety years, I have found that all pathways to learning begin with a story. Whether you talk about verbal/ linguistic intelligence (the ability to communicate through listening, reading, writing, and speaking) or other intelligences any psychologist can describe, you need first to *cultivate a will* to reach into your intelligence. Once that *will* surfaces, believe me, you will become *somebody*.

A Final Thought

Do you watch cable TV? Turner Classic Movies keep me fascinated. For the fifth time in my long life, I saw James Stewart and Jean Arthur playing in *Mr. Smith Goes to Washington*, where an idealist senator takes on political corruption. The movie ended with Stewart's character claiming his Senate bill could be a "lost cause."

Lord, let this not be my own "lost cause"! Show me <u>optimistic thinking</u> at its highest level.

Once again, dear reader, please e-mail <u>your</u> thoughts and ideas to **AllTheArts@yahoo.com**.

> NOTE: A condensed, revised chapter from **Chubby's Story** entitled "I Take Responsibility" will be sent to the first fifteen (15) individuals who e-mail their recommendations for getting all the arts in every school to **AllTheArts@yahoo.com**.

Biographies

Teresa deBarba-Miller

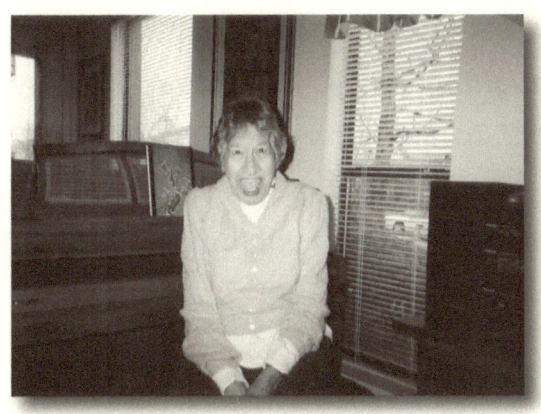

*This is Teresa at her piano, crowing after her first piano lesson in **April 2011! A lifelong dream.***

1988—With assistance from Anne Pellowski (edited by Norma Livo) and the cooperation of many professional storytellers, Teresa compiled a book entitled ***Joining In: An Anthology of Audience Participation Stories & How to Tell Them*** (Yellow Moon Press, Cambridge, MA), now in its ninth printing.

2006—***The ABC's of Real Health***, written to sell on the web. This went nowhere because the week copies arrived was the week a stroke hit her. Bold she may be, but she withheld offering the title, even after her recovery. (It's still a good book!)

2008—With twenty-eight (28) professional storytellers and expert help from the publishing editors, came ***Holiday Stories All Year Round: Audience Participation Stories and More Holiday Data*** (Libraries Unlimited).

2010—*CHUBBY'S STORY* (Cordon Publications). It took 390 pages to chronicle the wisdom and life lessons acquired through "87 years of living an improbable life." The book candidly talks about *life* and her solutions to many of the challenges we all face as we grow older.

2012—*Santa Claus in Laughing Valley: A Christmas Fantasy and a Call for Every Parent to Fight for the Arts in Public Schools.*

Teresa's books are available through the publisher or through Amazon.com.

Thomas Alden Morgan (Thomm)

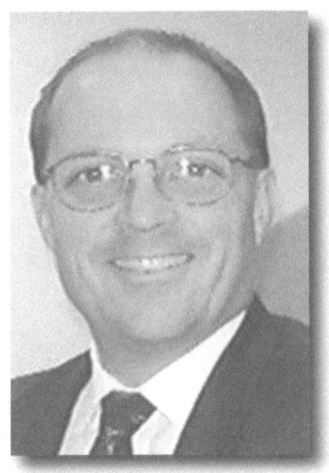 Thomm was trained as a journalist and editor during military service as a staff writer in the United States Air Force from 1984 to 1990.

At age 46, in March 2009, he was awarded MBA/public administration credentials to complement an associate degree in public affairs and policy earned in 1987. Thomm believes his thesis, "Microeconomic Growth during Macroeconomic Recession," should be a leading work on peaceful global economic reform and recovery.

Today, Thomm continues to freelance, editing manuscripts, writing advertising copy, designing marketing campaigns and promotional materials to support small business owners.

He is a member of Toastmasters International, is active in his church and community, and strives to advance his personal motto, "Live to serve, and serve to live." His personal vision for world change through managed philanthropy is published in the Internet at http://12Trillion.org.

Thomm lives in O'Fallon, Missouri, with his wife Caryn. They have four children.

Laura Simms

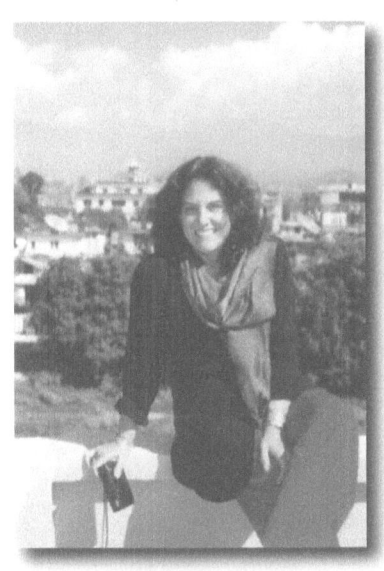

Laura Simms, senior research fellow for Rutgers-Newark, is an award-winning storyteller, recording artist, writer, educator, and humanitarian engaged in individual and community transformation. She is working with Mercy Corps Inc. in Haiti as a narrative therapist. She offers performances, keynotes, and workshops in conferences, villages, schools, universities, and community events worldwide. She is a member of the Therapeutic Arts Alliance Manhattan, a senior teacher of Shambhala Buddhist meditation. Among her notable awards are the Brimstone Award for Engaged Storytelling and *Sesame Street*'s award for work with children worldwide. She is co-faculty with Terry Tempest Williams at the University of Utah and works closely with ETSU Cancer Stories Project. She is a spoken-word consultant for the Alternative Arts High School in Portland, Oregon. Her most recent book is *Our Secret Territory: The Essence of Storytelling* (Sentient Books, June 2011). **www.laurasimms.com**

A Christmas Fantasy

—THE END—

No, really, this is the end.
Are you still reading?
Close the book!

www.ingramcontent.com/pod-product-compliance
Lightning Source LLC
Chambersburg PA
CBHW021548290526
45784CB00016B/2553